MOSES

HERE I AM!

Andy Robb

Copyright © 2001 John Hunt Publishing Ltd
Text © 2001 Andy Robb
Illustrations © 2001 Andy Robb.

ISBN 1-84298- 043-2

Design by Nautilus Design, UK

Scriptures quoted from the Good News Bible published by The Bible
Societies/HarperCollins Publishers Ltd., UK,
© American Bible Society,1966, 1971, 1976, 1992.

Write to:
John Hunt Publishing Ltd
46A West Street
Alresford
Hampshire
SO24 9AU
UK

The rights of Andy Robb as author and illustrator of this work have been
asserted in accordance with the Copyright, Designs and Patents Act 1988.

A CIP catalogue record for this book is available from the British Library.

Printed in Guernsey, Channel Islands

CONTENTS

Introduction

What's the most boring thing you can think of? Okay, now multiply it by a zillion.

That's how boring a lot of people think the Bible is. The funny thing is, most people who think the Bible's mega mind-numbingly boring have never even read it!

Crazy or what?!

Imagine turning down a triple whopper chicken, cheese and yoghurt burger with gherkin and custard relish just because you'd never tried it...

On second thoughts that wasn't such a good suggestion.

But you get my point?

I mean, I'll bet you didn't even know that the Bible's got adverts in it to tell people what's going to happen in the future or that it told people that the world was round thousands of years before we'd worked it out.

There's so much stuff in the Bible we won't be able to look at every bit of it but the bits we've chosen will hopefully make you start to realise that the Bible maybe isn't quite so boring as you thought.

Have fun!

So What's The Bible All About?

The Bible isn't just one whopping great book.

It's actually 66 not-quite-so-whopping great books all whacked together like a sort of mini library.

The first book in the Bible is called Genesis, which was also the name of a pop group your parents once liked but they won't admit to it even if you hang them from the ceiling by their toenails...
and the last book is called Revelation which as far as I know wasn't the name of a pop group your parents once liked.

To keep things simple, the Bible is mainly about two things.
God.
And people.

Some interesting questions.

Who exactly wrote the Bible?
People.

Who decided what to write about?
God.

So how did they know what God wanted them to write?
Did God send an e-mail?

Er, not quite.
Here's one way of looking at it.
Imagine two people in love.

Enough of that!
Sorry, have I put you off your lunch?
When people are in love with each other all they want to do is
spend every waking hour gazing lovingly into each other's eyes.
(I know, it's horrible, isn't it!)

The way they hug and cuddle each other you wonder whether they've been permanently super-glued to each other for all eternity.

It even gets to the point where they start to think each other's thoughts.

Well, that's sort of what it was like for the guys who wrote the Bible (without the cuddling bit).

They spent so much time with God that they got to know what he was thinking and what he wanted to say.

Sometimes God even spoke to them in dreams or gave them visions of what he wanted to say.

I THINK HIS EXCUSE THAT HE OVERSLEEPS SO THAT GOD CAN SPEAK TO HIM IN DREAMS IS WEARING A BIT THIN!

They were totally in touch with God so that what they wrote was as if God had written it himself.

So what sort of things does God want to say to us?

For starters, the Bible tells us that there is a God and that he made you and me and the whole universe.

It also tells us that he wants us to be his friends and how we can do that.

What good is a book that was written *even before* my mum and dad were born? People might not wear silly costumes like they did in the past but God hasn't changed a bit, so what he had to say to people with funny headdresses and sandals thousands of years ago is still important for us.

The first two Boring Bible books *Ballistic Beginnings* and *Hotchpotch Hebrews* were both taken from just one book of the Bible - GENESIS.
This Boring Bible book is taken from *four* different books so it looks like we've got our work cut out
cramming it all in, but we'll have a go!
The four Bible books are called **EXODUS, LEVITICUS, NUMBERS AND DEUTERONOMY** but don't worry if you forget them, it's what God does in these stories that's really important.
So, let's stop wasting any more time and get cracking!

(By the way, I was only joking about hanging your parents upside down by their toenails - nose hairs work much better!!!)

In the last Boring Bible book, *Hotchpotch Hebrews*, the story ended with our hero, Joseph, becoming second-in-command to the Egyptian Pharaoh (nice move, Joseph!) and then bringing all his family to live with him in Egypt so that they wouldn't die of starvation in the famine that was sweeping the region.

Joseph's eleven brothers had planned to go back to the land of Canaan once things got better but somehow they never quite got round to making the return trip.

They saw out their days, along with Joseph, in the land of Egypt.

Perhaps the weather was nicer there, who knows?

Just in case you didn't know, Joseph's family wasn't any old family.

No way!

Their ancestor, Abraham, had been hand-picked by God to start a brand new nation that worshipped him and did exactly what he said.

For many years they were known as the 'Hebrews' but, as time passed, they gradually came to be called the 'Israelites' which is what *we're* going to call them in this book, if that's okay with you?

It's now coming up for nearly 400 years since the Israelites first settled in Egypt and right at the start of Exodus, the Bible says that the Israelites had increased in numbers so much so that they filled the land.

That was the *good* news.
The *bad* news was that they now had a *new* Pharaoh ruling the land.

(Pharaoh was simply another name for an Egyptian king.)

This Pharaoh knew nothing about Joseph and how he'd managed to save Egypt from dying of hunger when the famine had struck.

As far as he was concerned, the large number of Israelites living in Egypt was simply a bit of a nuisance that he could well do without.

To be honest, what he was *really* worried about was if the Israelites suddenly turned on him.

Right through history nations have been going to war against one another and in those ancient times it was no exception.

If the Egyptians weren't invading a near neighbour then you could almost guarantee someone was trying to attack *them*.

All it needed was the Israelites to take sides with an invading army and the Egyptians would be finished.

This new Pharaoh wasn't going to take any chances.

There was only one thing for it.

The Israelites had to be made into slaves.

Take away their freedom, put slave masters over them and set them to work for the Pharaoh, that was the plan and that's what they did.

**Boring Bible Fact: Slavery wasn't common in Egypt.
It wasn't until the Egyptians started to conquer foreign
lands and bring back their inhabitants as captives that they
began to use slave labour.**

Unfortunately for Pharaoh, things didn't go the way he planned.
The harder he made it for the Israelite slaves, the more their
numbers seem to grow.

The funny thing was, according to the Bible, the Egyptians came
to dread the Israelites, even
though *they* were their slaves.
The *Israelites* didn't find
anything funny about their
present circumstances.

The Bible says that they were well
and truly cheesed-off with the
way things were going.
(Well, it doesn't exactly say
'cheesed-off' but you know what I mean!)
The Egyptians were cruel and harsh task masters and made the
Israelites' life a misery.

What Sort Of Work Did Pharaoh Force The Israelites To Do?

One thing that kings are *especially* fond of is building things so that people remember them even when they're dead and gone. Pharaoh was no exception.

He had set about a major programme of building throughout the land which included store cities in Rameses and Pithom.

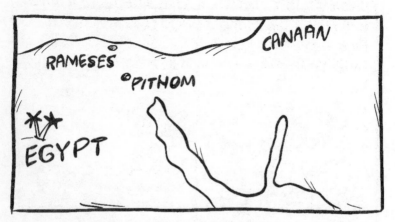

In those days they didn't have mechanical diggers and cranes to do all the hard work so if you wanted to build anything on a large scale you were going to need thousands upon thousands of labourers to do all your hard work.

There's a stroke of luck! That's precisely what the Pharaoh had with his Israelite slaves.

To do any sort of building you needed either stone or bricks, so bricks is what the Israelites made.

Fascinating Fact:

Archaeologists have unearthed fragments of pottery in Egypt on which building supervisors scribbled notes just like you would on a memo pad. They record the daily details of building projects from around the time we are looking at in Exodus.

Here are some of the reasons for workers being absent...

You would have thought that Pharaoh would have been grateful for the increase in the Israelite population, but nothing of the sort.

More Israelite slaves should have meant more people to accomplish his building projects.

But fearing that they would rebel against him drove Pharaoh to his next terrible plan.

Pharaoh summoned Shiphrah and Puah, the Israelite midwives who helped the Israelite women to give birth and commanded them to do something really dreadful.

The midwives must have been scared stiff of Pharaoh but the Bible says that they feared God more.
They disobeyed Pharaoh and let the Israelite boys live.
Pharaoh was none-too-pleased.

God protected Shiphrah and Puah from Pharaoh's anger and Pharaoh went back to the drawing board to think of what else he could do.

Then, at long last, Pharaoh conjured up his most dastardly plan yet.

Boring Bible Tricky Question

What would *you* do if you were an Israelite living in Egypt and you'd just had a baby boy?

Would you throw it into the River Nile and watch it drown before your eyes or would you disobey Pharaoh?

If you thought that disobeying Pharaoh was the best option then you wouldn't have been alone.

One Israelite woman did just that.

When her baby boy was three months old, and when she couldn't hide him any longer, she got a papyrus basket for him, coated it in tar and pitch (to make it waterproof) and put it among the reeds by the bank of the River Nile.

The baby's sister stood at a distance to see what would would happen to her brother.

Boring Bible Fact: Papyrus baskets were made from papyrus reeds taken from the river bank.

The baby's sister didn't have long to wait as she lurked in the undergrowth.

Who should turn up but Pharaoh's daughter along with her attendants.

Seeing the basket among the reeds she immediately sent her slave-girl to fetch it.

The reed basket must have had a lid on it because the Bible says that Pharaoh's daughter opened it.

Quite a lot is known about Pharaoh's daughter.

For starters her name was Princess Hatshepsut, as far as we know, and she was probably about seventeen years old when she discovered the baby in the basket.

Hatshepsut eventually became one of the most powerful and feared of all Egypt's rulers. Even before she actually became Queen she had great influence over the Pharaohs, the first of whom was her father who was completely dominated by her. Such was her power that her nephew, one of Egypt's later Pharaohs, absolutely hated her.

For all that, she must have been a bit of a softy when it came to babies because the Bible says that she felt sorry for the little crying baby she'd rescued from the Nile.

The baby's sister was a pretty smart young girl.
Pretending to be a passer-by, she approached the Pharaoh's daughter and asked...

Knowing that the baby was an Israelite, Pharaoh's daughter agreed to the idea.

Bet you can't guess who the sister fetched to nurse the baby? Yep, you guessed it, his own mother.

Pharoah's daughter wasn't stupid either.

She waited until the baby was well past pooing its nappies and being sick everywhere before she had the boy brought to the royal palace to live with her as her own child.

Hatshepsut gave the boy a name...

Boring Bible Fact: In the Hebrew language, Moses sounds like the word for *draw out*.

Life As A Prince

Moses had well and truly fallen on his feet.
One minute he's living as the child of a slave family and the next he's being treated like royalty.
As an Egyptian prince, Moses would have had the finest education in the land.

Boring Bible Joke:
What were Pharaoh's favourite photos?
Moses PRINTS of Egypt!

Nowadays we take it for granted that we are taught to read and write but in ancient Egypt only the privileged few would have learnt these skills.

The Egyptians were also excellent mathematicians, so Moses, like many others in the land, would have had all the skills necessary to do all the complicated calculations needed to build their vast cities.

Growing up in the royal palace would probably have meant that Moses had servants of his very own to attend to his every whim and need.
What a difference from his early years when he almost ended up being drowned in the Nile.

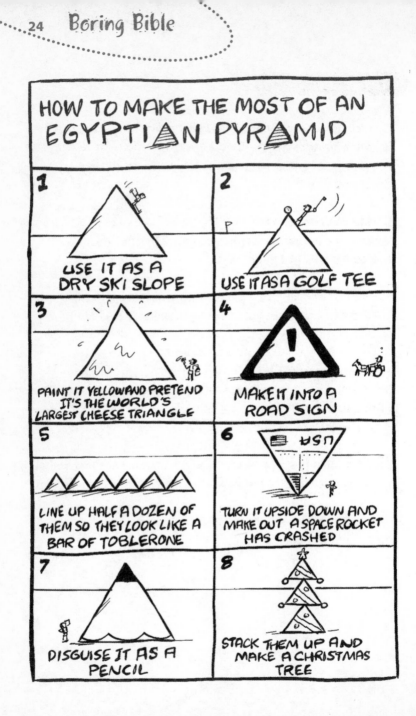

HOW TO MAKE THE MOST OF AN EGYPTIAN PYRAMID

1 USE IT AS A DRY SKI SLOPE

2 USE IT AS A GOLF TEE

3 PAINT IT YELLOW AND PRETEND IT'S THE WORLD'S LARGEST CHEESE TRIANGLE

4 MAKE IT INTO A ROAD SIGN

5 LINE UP HALF A DOZEN OF THEM SO THEY LOOK LIKE A BAR OF TOBLERONE

6 TURN IT UPSIDE DOWN AND MAKE OUT A SPACE ROCKET HAS CRASHED

7 DISGUISE IT AS A PENCIL

8 STACK THEM UP AND MAKE A CHRISTMAS TREE

Fascinating Fact:

Historians from the distant past tell us that Moses, along with his adoptive mother, were responsible for leading the Egyptian armies into many great battles.

Later in Exodus we will find out how Moses once again uses his skills as a leader but this time it's not the Egyptian army he's leading!

Although Moses grew up as an Egyptian prince, he never forgot the Israelite people he had come from.
One day, when Moses was a man, he went out to the place where the Israelite slaves were working.
The work of a slave was very, very hard.
Moses must have been heartbroken to see his own people treated so harshly.
The final straw came when he saw one of the Egyptian slave-drivers beating an Israelite slave.
Checking to see that no-one was looking, Moses killed the Egyptian and then buried him in the sand.

I don't know about you, but I think Moses would have made a good wrestling referee because the very next day he was back in action trying to break up a fight - between two Israelites this time.

The Israelites didn't take too kindly to Moses poking his nose into other people's business.

Moses realised that the game was up.

Word had obviously got around that he'd killed an Egyptian slave-driver and who knows what would become of him.

Would he be sent to prison?

Would he be sentenced to death?

Could Pharaoh's daughter protect him from being punished by the Pharaoh?

Moses couldn't risk it.

There's was only one thing left to do...

SCRAM!

And a good job he did too!

Moses was dead right about Pharaoh.

Hatshepsut might have had a soft spot for her adopted Israelite son but when the Pharaoh found out what Moses had done he tried to have him killed.

Moses hot-footed it to Midian.

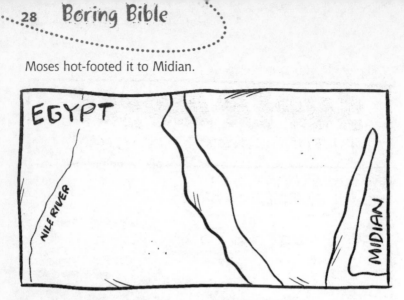

As you can see, Midian was bit of trek, but Moses probably wanted to put a lot of distance between him and the fuming Pharaoh.

Boring Bible Fact: The Midianites who lived in the land of Midian, were, like Moses, descendants of Abraham so Moses would have felt very much at home with them.

The seven girls were all the daughters of the priest of Midian. They were full of it when they returned home.

They told their father of how an Egyptian (or so they thought), had come to their rescue and how he'd kindly watered their flock.

Moses was invited to come and stay with the family as a special guest which was a much better prospect than wandering around in the desert like he'd done for the last little while.

Mrs Moses

Moses and Zipporah, one of the seven daughters, got married. In time they had a son who they called Gershom.

The tent-dwelling Midianites had become his family and life in Egypt was now a thing of the past.

The years went by...

...and the Pharaoh who was out to get Moses died.

BYE!

Moses spent his days in the desert tending his father-in-law's flock.

2 YEAR

Let's be honest, looking after your flocks day in, day out must have been just a teensy bit boring but I'll bet even Moses wouldn't have chosen to liven things up in the way that happened next.

As Moses came to Sinai, which the Bible calls the holy mountain, something strange appeared before his eyes.
A bush was on fire.
But it wasn't burning up.
How peculiar.
Moses approached it to take a closer look.
As Moses edged closer, the mystery became clear.
This was no ordinary fire.
Suddenly a voice called to him from within the bush.

It was a bright and fiery angel of God speaking to him.

Boring Bible Fact: Angels are God's messengers sent to do his work and to tell people what he wants them to hear. It's as if God was speaking through the angels.

Moses was so frightened he daren't even look at the bush.

Boring Bible Poser

If you were Moses, what would *you* do?

1 Run away from the burning bush as fast as your legs could carry you?
2 Suggest someone better qualified to do the job?
3 Remind God that you'd had to do a runner from Egypt because you'd killed someone so going back probably wouldn't be such a good idea?
4 Say you'd think about it and you'll get back to God when you've made up your mind?
5 Jump at the chance to be a hero again?
6 Come up with lots of excuses why you wouldn't be the best man for the job?
7 Say "No"?

Let's check out what *Moses* did.

WHO AM I THAT I SHOULD GO TO PHARAOH AND BRING THE ISRAELITES OUT OF EGYPT?

Yep! He *still* wasn't convinced God had picked the right man.
Then God did something really amazing.
He made a promise to Moses to persuade him that he would be with him every step of the way.
God promised that once the Israelites were free they would come back to Sinai to worship him.

Tough luck, but you're going to have to wait to find out whether or not God *did* keep his promise to Moses and whether the Israelites eventually worshipped God on the holy mountain.

One thing's for sure, if they *didn't* then God was not with them.

You'd think that Moses would have been a bit more confident knowing that God was going to be with him all the way.
Not a bit of it.
Moses was still scared stiff and who's to say that you and I wouldn't be as well if we were standing in his shoes, or should I say sandals?

Excuses, Excuses!

Here's a list of all the excuses Moses made for *not* going back to Egypt.

1 Who am I to do such a big job?
2 They might not know who my God is.
3 They might not believe me.
4 They might not listen to me.
5 I'm not a good speaker.
6 Can't you send someone else?

The Bible tells us that Moses, constant excuses made God angry but amazingly he still wanted Moses to do the job.

WHAT ABOUT YOUR BROTHER, AARON? **HE** CAN SPEAK WELL. **HE** WILL SPEAK TO THE PEOPLE **FOR** YOU.

Sorted!
At *last*!

Boring Bible Joke:
How do we know that Moses wore a wig?
Because the Bible says that Moses had 'AIR ON to speak!

Time To Say Goodbye

Moses went back to Jethro, his father-in-law, and asked to be allowed to return to Egypt.

Jethro sent him with his blessing.

Along with his wife and sons, Moses headed back to Egypt. Moses made sure to pack his special staff.

Somehow he just knew he was going to be needing it.

Hang On A Minute...

Why was God so keen to set the *Israelites* free from slavery. What had *they* done to deserve special treatment?

I'll bet there were plenty of other nations who were suffering in similar ways.

Why didn't God send someone to free *them*?

That's a good question.

If you've read Boring Bible books *Ballistic Beginnings* and *Hotchpotch Hebrews* then you'll probably remember how God made two people, Adam and Eve, to look after the world, to have children and most importantly of all to love the God who had made them.

The bad news was that Adam and Eve blew it by disobeying God.

That meant their friendship with him was broken and God's perfect creation was spoiled.

Although people continued to turn their backs on the God who had made them and loved them, God didn't abandon *them*. It was always in *his* heart to give people the chance to be his friends once again.

But he needed some people to help him with his plan.

He required a nation of people whom he could show his love to and who could be taught how to live lives that pleased him. These people were the Israelites and if God left them to die as slaves in Egypt then his plan to use them to show the *whole* world that he loved them and cared for them would be completely ruined.

Moses' mission to free the Israelite slaves was also going to be part of God's bigger plan to give the rest of the world the chance be his friends once again.

Back To Egypt

Before Moses reached Egypt, God had arranged for him to meet up with his brother, Aaron, back at Sinai, the mountain of God. We can only guess that even while Moses was being brought up as an Egyptian prince he'd kept in touch with his *real* Israelite family so that he and Aaron weren't complete strangers when they met up at Sinai.

Moses filled Aaron in with all that God had told him, including the miraculous signs.

On their arrival in Egypt the brothers brought together all the Israelite leaders and gave them the low-down on what God had said and what he was planning to do.
Just to make sure they believed him, Moses performed the miraculous signs that God had shown him.

The Israelite leaders, full of wonder at God's goodness, bowed down and worshipped God.

Well, that was the first bit over with for Moses.
It'll bet that it wasn't as bad as he'd thought it would be.
At least they didn't tell him to clear off back to Midian.
Now for the tricky part.
Meeting Pharaoh.

Just for one moment imagine that you've been given the opportunity to go and meet with someone like the President of the United States or the Queen of England.
Sounds great doesn't it?
Now, imagine that instead of going to have a nice, polite little chat with them about nothing in particular you're going to tell them something they *don't* want to hear like...

> I'M AFRAID THAT YOU'RE GOING TO HAVE TO START PAYING CHILDREN FOR GOING TO SCHOOL, OTHERWISE GOD WILL PUNISH YOU !

or...

> LET EVERYONE HAVE A LIE-IN ON MONDAY MORNINGS OR YOU'RE GOING TO BE FOR IT !

or...

>

Fill this speech bubble in yourself.

To tell the truth, saying something like that might make you a
bit unpopular but it's hardly going to get you executed.
Not so with a tyrannical ruler like the Pharaoh.
He had power to let you live or die.
An audience with Pharaoh wouldn't have been on Moses and
Aaron's top ten list of 'Things I Like Doing Best'.

Here Goes...

THIS IS WHAT THE LORD, THE GOD OF ISRAEL SAYS...
'LET MY PEOPLE GO, SO THAT THEY MAY HOLD
A FESTIVAL IN THE DESERT TO HONOUR ME'.

So far, so good...

Oh dear!
It doesn't look like it's going quite to plan.

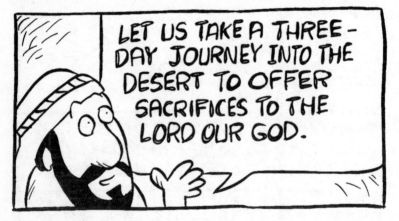

Yeah, good idea, Moses! If he won't let the Israelites go for good then perhaps Pharaoh will at least let them take a short holiday.

Um, er... well, Moses and Aaron, there's not really a lot you can say to *that*, is there?

Fascinating Fact:

It is believed that Queen Hatshepsut, who adopted Moses as a baby, built a temple for Moses and the Israelites at a place called Serabit, which was a three-day journey from Egypt.

This new Pharaoh probably knew nothing of this Israelite privilege which Moses was probably trying to re-introduce with his request to the Pharaoh. No doubt Pharaoh just thought they would use it as an excuse to escape.

Archaeologists (that's people who study things left behind by people from the past) discovered this interesting stone tablet in Queen Hatshepsut's temple at Serabit.

Just in case you don't understand Egyptian, we've translated it for you.

Here's what it says...

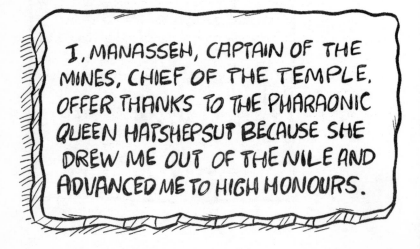

I, MANASSEH, CAPTAIN OF THE MINES, CHIEF OF THE TEMPLE, OFFER THANKS TO THE PHARAONIC QUEEN HATSHEPSUT BECAUSE SHE DREW ME OUT OF THE NILE AND ADVANCED ME TO HIGH HONOURS.

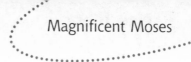

What does all *that* mean?

Well, for a start, Manasseh was actually Moses in *Hebrew*.

It also tells us that the person mentioned was pulled out of the Nile by Queen Hatshepsut.

So, what we've got here is an inscription that's all about none other than our hero, Moses.

What a find!

Back to the story.

You're possibly asking why Moses only asked Pharaoh if the Israelites could go on a short round-trip to worship God rather than actually just leave the country for good.

In all probability, God was testing Pharaoh to see how hard his heart was towards the Israelites over a simple request.

If he wasn't going to let them do *this* then no way would he let them go permanently.

From Pharaoh's response it was obvious that he was going to be totally unresponsive to Moses and Aaron's pleas.

The Bible says that the Israelite slaves scattered all over Egypt to gather stubble to use for straw. Seems a bit unfair to me but then Pharaoh was hardly the most reasonable sort of chap, was he?

When the slaves didn't meet their quotas, the Pharaoh had the Israelite foremen beaten.

Things were getting so desperate that they even appealed to Pharaoh.

Look Out Moses!

The Israelite foremen knew *exactly* who to blame for the way things had turned out.

But they weren't in the mood for any sort of explanation. They were furious.

Moses was at a loss to know what to do or say.

God said...

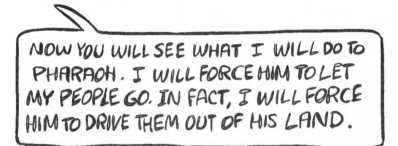

Moses took this good news back to the Israelite slaves but they didn't want to hear what he had to say. As far as they were concerned, Moses was *bad* news.

Things weren't looking too good for Moses.
The Israelites now loathed him, Pharaoh was against him and God was still insistent that he stuck to his guns.
Bet he wished he was back tending the flocks in Midian.
Anything must have been better than having to go back to Pharaoh again.

Boring Bible Fact: Moses was 83 years old when God told him to go back to Egypt.

As Moses and Aaron went before Pharaoh once more, God had told them that it was time to let Pharaoh know who was boss.

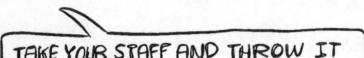

TAKE YOUR STAFF AND THROW IT DOWN BEFORE PHARAOH AND IT WILL BECOME A SNAKE.

Here goes nothing...

Would you believe it? Of all the sneaky tricks, Pharaoh's sorcerers managed to use their magic powers to produce a snake of their own.

The Bible says that because of this Pharaoh now became even more stubborn and refused, point blank, to listen to Moses and Aaron.

It was now time for God to tighten the screws on Pharaoh.

God was now preparing to loosen Pharaoh's grip on his Israelite slaves, bit by bit, by inflicting on the Egyptians a series of increasingly terrible plagues.

Strike One

God told Moses to go and
meet Pharaoh at the banks
of the Nile and command
him to let the Israelites go.

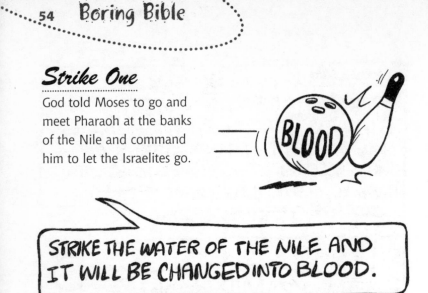

STRIKE THE WATER OF THE NILE AND
IT WILL BE CHANGED INTO BLOOD.

God also instructed Aaron to hold out his staff over all the rivers,
ponds, reservoirs and canals and they would turn to blood as
well.

All the fish died and the place stunk something rotten but

I THINK WE'VE TAKEN
A WRONG TURNING.
THIS LOOKS LIKE
THE **RED** SEA!

because stubborn old Pharaoh's magicians were able to do the
same thing he refused to change his mind about freeing the
Israelites.

Strike Two

One week later, Moses was back before Pharaoh asking him once again to let the Israelites go.
Pharaoh's reply was the same as always...

Aaron stretched out his hand over all the streams, ponds and canals in Egypt and out of them came a hideous plague of frogs that covered the land.
Pharaoh tried to outdo Moses and Aaron's God by getting his magicians to conjure up their own frogs but that only made things worse with even more frogs hopping and croaking all over the land.

Pharaoh eventually had to ask Moses to pray to God to get rid of the frogs. His magicians couldn't do *that*. God answered Moses' prayer and the frogs died.

But *still* he wouldn't let the Israelites go.

Strike Three

Then God said to Moses...

TELL AARON, "STRETCH OUT YOUR STAFF AND STRIKE THE DUST OF THE GROUND" AND THROUGHOUT THE LAND OF EGYPT THE DUST WILL BECOME GNATS.

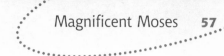

This next plague was as bad as the last.
Horrible, itchy gnats everywhere.
In your hair, in your food, in your drinking water.

Gnats were something even Pharaoh's magicians couldn't reproduce.

The Bible tells us that even Pharaoh was honest enough to recognise that this was an act of God but because of his hard heart he still wouldn't let the Israelites go.

Fascinating Fact:

*The Egyptians believed that their Pharaoh was a god
and it was in his power to make sure the world ran
smoothly. For him to acknowledge that there was another
God more powerful than himself was quite an admission!*

Strike Four

Next it was the turn of a
plague of flies to do its stuff
on Pharaoh.
The Bible says that Moses
got up early in the morning
and confronted Pharaoh.

THE LORD SAYS, "LET MY PEOPLE GO SO THAT THEY MAY WORSHIP ME. IF YOU DON'T LET MY PEOPLE GO, I WILL SEND SWARMS OF FLIES ON YOU AND YOUR OFFICIALS, ON YOUR PEOPLE AND INTO YOUR HOUSES. THE HOUSES OF THE EGYPTIANS WILL BE FULL OF FLIES AND EVEN ON THE GROUND WHERE THEY ARE!"

Just as Moses promised, God sent a devastating plague of flies on Egypt which ruined the land.

Amazingly, God prevented the plague from affecting his people, the Israelites who lived in the nearby land of Goshen.

Pharaoh was at his wits' end.

No go!

Moses knew what sort of reaction he'd get from the Egyptians.

They'd be so appalled at the sight of animals being slaughtered and sacrificed that they'd turn on the Israelites.

Many of the Egyptian gods

were represented by animals and to kill what to them was a sacred animal was a terrible thing to do.

No, it had to be a three-day journey into the desert or nothing.

At long last, Pharaoh relented.

Once again, at Pharaoh's request, Moses prayed to God for the plague to be removed.

As soon as the flies were gone, guess what Pharaoh did?

You're right, he changed his mind yet again!

Boring Bible Fact: Not one of God's punishing plagues touched his people, the Israelites, the whole time.

WELL, FOLKS, THAT'S FOUR BALLS PLAYED FOR THE ISRAELITES AND THEY'VE ALL BEEN DIRECT HITS BUT AT THIS STAGE OF THE GAME THE EGYPTIANS ARE IN NO MOOD FOR GIVING UP.

God kept sending plague after plague onto Egypt to make Pharaoh let the Israelites go but Pharaoh just kept on changing his mind and making excuses.

Strike Five

Next, God struck down every Egyptian horse, donkey, camel, sheep, goat and cow with sickness so they died,

Not one animal belonging to the Egyptians was left alive.

Strike Six

Then, God infected the entire Egyptian nation with an awful plague of boils (ooch, nasty), but *still* Pharaoh remained as stubborn as ever and would not release his Israelite slaves.

Strike Seven

The seventh plague that God visited upon
Egypt was dreadful.
The worst hailstorm in Egypt's
history ripped through the land
destroying anything and
everything that got in its way.
It was the most devastating experi-
ence you could imagine,
wiping out crops and people alike.
But would Pharaoh heed God?
Not on your life.
He just dug his heels in further.

Strike Eight

As if the Egyptians hadn't had
enough of insects the next plague
that God was about to send was
locusts.

But could Egypt cope with any more
destruction?

Had the time come for Pharaoh to finally give in to Moses'
demands?

HANG ON, FOLKS, IT LOOKS LIKE
THE GAME MIGHT BE OVER. THE
EGYPTIAN TEAM ARE HAVING A
TEAM TALK AS WE SPEAK. IT
LOOKS LIKE THEY'VE HAD ENOUGH
OF GOD'S PLAGUES AND ARE
GOING TO THROW IN
THE TOWEL.

Has Pharaoh finally given in to pressure from God? Will he, at long last, let the Israelites go to worship God in the desert?

It was all or nothing as far as God was concerned.
It wasn't up to Pharaoh to pick and choose who went to worship God and who didn't.

God commanded Moses to stretch out his hand over Egypt so that locusts swarmed over the land.

Locusts so great in number that they covered every inch of the land.

Locusts so great in number that they devoured everything in their path.

Locusts so great in number that they filled every Egyptian home.

Strike Nine

For three long days, the whole of Egypt was plunged into thick, black darkness by God. Except for the Israelites, that is.

The places *they* lived in still had light.

GO, WORSHIP THE LORD. EVEN YOUR WOMEN AND CHILDREN MAY GO WITH YOU BUT LEAVE YOUR FLOCKS AND HERDS BEHIND!

Oops!
Slight problem...

OUR LIVESTOCK MUST GO TOO! WE HAVE TO USE SOME OF THEM TO WORSHIP GOD AND UNTIL WE GET THERE WE WON'T KNOW WHICH ONES WE'LL NEED.

Pharaoh was not going to change his mind.
In fact, he'd had it up to *here* with the Israelites...

God had one more card to play to make absolutely certain that
Pharaoh let the Israelites go free.

The Strategy

Tell all the Israelites to take a lamb.........
(small households can share one)..............
The lamb must be one year old and without
defect...
Two weeks from today, at twilight, slaughter the
lambs......................................
Smear the lambs' blood on the tops and sides of
the door-frames. That same night, eat the meat
with bitter herbs and bread made without yeast.
Do not leave anything until morning........Tuck
your cloak into your belt, eat quickly and get
ready to leave in haste..... This is the Lord's
Passover....................................
This night I will pass through Egypt and kill
every firstborn - men and animals.............
When I see the blood on your house I will pass
over you....................................
No destructive plague will touch you when I
strike Egypt.

**Boring Bible Fact: Each part of the Passover meal
represented something different.**
**The lamb or kid spoke of God's protection for Israel which he
called his firstborn.**
**The bitter herbs were a reminder to the Israelites of all the
bitter years of slavery.**
**The bread without yeast represented their quick departure
from Egypt and the fact that there wasn't time to use yeast
and wait for the bread to rise.**
**From that day to this, the Israelite nation still celebrates the
Passover Feast to remember this great moment in
history.**

Strike Ten

The time had finally come for God to inflict his last terrible plague on the evil Pharaoh.
As night fell, the Israelite people carried out all that God had commanded them to do and then waited.

Who knows what was going through their minds?

Were they scared that God would strike down *their* firstborn as well?

How well did they know the God of their ancestors Abraham, Isaac and Jacob?

Could he be trusted?

Had they really given him the worship he required?

It was too late to do anything now.

All they could do was sit it out.

At the stroke of midnight, the Bible tells us that God struck down all the firstborn of Egypt right from the firstborn of Pharaoh to the firstborn of the prisoner in the dungeon. Pharaoh and all his officials awoke during the night to the awful loud wailing of Egypt mourning its dead.

Pharaoh summoned Moses and Aaron...

It took the death of his own firstborn son to force Pharaoh to finally release his Israelite slaves.

THAT'S TEN STRIKES FOR THE ISRAELITES AND THEY'VE WON THEIR FREEDOM. WHO'D HAVE THOUGHT THAT THE GAME WOULD END WITH SUCH A CRUSHING DEFEAT FOR THE EGYPTIANS AND A RESOUNDING VICTORY FOR THE ISRAELITE UNDERDOGS? I SUPPOSE THAT'S WHAT'S HAPPENS WHEN YOU'VE GOT GOD ON YOUR TEAM. BYE FOR NOW!

Fascinating Fact:

Archaeologists have made a most astounding discovery at the foot of the Sphinx statue outside Cairo. When the sand was cleared away between its paws a 14-foot high, red granite memorial stone was found. The inscription on it said that Pharaoh's eldest son (his firstborn) did not come to the throne as expected because of his sudden death but his younger brother did instead.

This happened at around 1440BC, the same time as the Bible tells us the Israelites left Egypt. So history confirms what the Bible says, that even Pharaoh's eldest son was struck down by God in this last judgement.

I'll bet the Egyptian people were glad to see the back of the Israelites after all the plagues they'd had to endure.

That must have been why, as the Bible tells us, they gave the Israelites silver, gold and clothing to take with them.

I'M AFRAID THAT YOU'RE GOING TO HAVE TO PAY US A BIT MORE THAN **THAT**! BEING A SLAVE FOR 400 YEARS DOESN'T COME CHEAP!

In fact, the Israelites had lived in Egypt for 430 years to the very day though they'd only actually been slaves for 400 of those years!

Fascinating Fact:

Back in the book of Genesis, God had already told Abraham that the Israelites would be slaves in a foreign land for a period of 400 years!

It must have been quite a sight as the entire Israelite population upped and left the land of Egypt.

The Bible says that there were about 600,000 men, let alone women and children.

What we're looking at here is something in the region of **two million** people beside all their cattle, flocks and herds heading out of slavery.

Moses didn't need to worry about planning their journey, God had already done that for him.

The *shortest* route would have been *this* way...

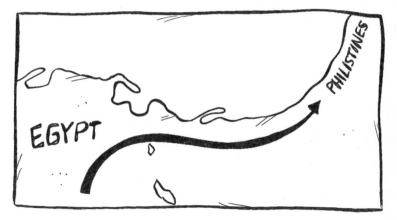

...but God knew that they would have to pass through the land of the Philistines and that could mean having to go to war against them to get through.

Any sign of trouble would have been enough to make the Israelites have second thoughts and go straight back to Egypt. If it was a choice between being enslaved by the Egyptians or killed by the Philistines then slavery won hands down every time.

So, God led them out into the desert, the *long* way round...

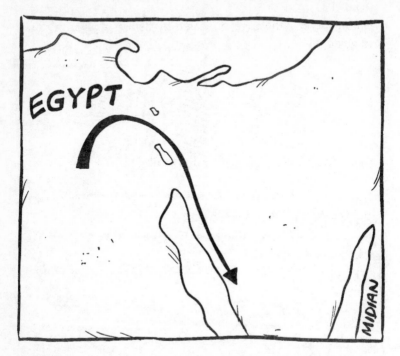

Did You Know....that the word 'Exodus', (which is the name of this Bible book) simply means 'departure?

Now, you might well be asking how exactly God led the Israelites.
Did he...

a Put up road signs along the route?
b Call out the directions from heaven?
c Give Moses a map?
d Send an angel to lead them?

The correct answer is d).

An angel from God went before them but in a most unusual manner.

During the day, the angel appeared to them as a pillar of cloud to guide them...

...and during the night he went before them as a pillar of fire to lead them.

That meant that they could travel both night *and* day and not waste any time escaping from the clutches of the evil Pharaoh.

Oops! Me and my big mouth. That rotten old Pharaoh really *is* a nasty piece of work. You'll never guess what he's gone and done? He's gone and changed his mind.

WHAT HAVE WE **DONE**? WE HAVE LET THE ISRAELITES GO AND LOST THEIR SERVICES!

How could Pharaoh have forgotten God's terrible punishing plagues in such a short space of time?

It just goes to show how hard-hearted he really was.

Pharaoh wasted no time in dispatching 600 of his best chariots along with all the other chariots and troops of Egypt in pursuit of the unsuspecting Israelites.

Meanwhile the Israelites had camped here...

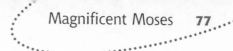

Yikes!

Just as the Israelites were making themselves comfy by the sea shore they looked up and saw Mr Meany himself, the Pharaoh, approaching...

...followed by thousands upon thousands of Egyptian troops!

Three Choices

I wonder what you'd do if you were one of the Israelites.

Would you try and pretend that you *weren't* the Israelites at all?

Would you trust God to come to your rescue?

Or would you just panic?

After much consideration, the Israelites decided that in the circumstances and all things considered, they'd probably be best going for option number three.
So they did!

But Moses stood his ground.
He wasn't going to panic.
Over the years Moses had seen God do some amazing things.

Maybe that's what was running through his mind as the
Egyptian army advanced on them.

God had always been faithful and trustworthy and Moses knew
in his heart that God was not going to desert them now, in their
hour of need.

DO NOT BE AFRAID! STAND FIRM AND YOU WILL SEE THE DELIVERANCE THE LORD WILL BRING YOU TODAY. THE EGYPTIANS YOU SEE TODAY YOU WILL NEVER SEE AGAIN. THE LORD WILL FIGHT FOR YOU... YOU ONLY NEED TO BE STILL!

Now it was *God's* turn to do something.
As the Egyptian army advanced closer upon the trapped
Israelites, the pillar of cloud that had been leading them up
front moved behind the Israelites and came between them and
the Egyptians.
The Egyptian army was immediately plunged into darkness
while the Israelites still had light even when night fell.

Then God spoke to Moses...

RAISE YOUR STAFF AND STRETCH OUT YOUR HAND OVER THE SEA TO DIVIDE THE WATER SO THAT THE ISRAELITES CAN GO THROUGH ON DRY GROUND.

Moses did as God commanded and a strong east wind blew all night long, dividing the waters of the Red Sea with a wall of water on either side and drying up the sea bed so it could be crossed in safety.

A Bridge Too Far

Wherever you travel in the world you come across bridges of all shapes and sizes that enable people to cross even the widest of rivers.

One of the most impressive structures is the Golden Gate bridge in San Francisco. It spans a ginormous 1,280 metres.

Sometimes the distance between one side and the other is *so* big that it's necessary to dig a tunnel *under* the river to cross it. It's not just river banks that are linked by tunnels.

Sometimes even countries are.

Between Britain and France runs the Channel Tunnel carrying people and transport for 31 miles under the sea.

All of these structures, be they bridges or tunnels, took many years to build.

Moses and the Israelites didn't have that sort of time on their hands.

It was now or never.

Not a bridge, not a tunnel but a pathway right through the *middle* of the sea. Wow!

What might have taken men many years to achieve, God did in just one night.

Wagons Roll!

As dawn approached, Moses gave the Israelites the signal to move.

It must have been an awesome sight walking through that huge corridor of water wondering whether it wouldn't suddenly come crashing down on top of you.

All the while, the Egyptians were unaware of what was happening the other side of the pillar of cloud.

With the Israelites almost across we can only but guess that God must have allowed the Egyptians to see what was going on. They mounted their chariots and pursued the escaping Israelites. Perhaps they should have checked out whether Egyptian armies were allowed to use God's miraculous pathway before they hurtled across it.

As they raced through the tunnel of water God threw the Egyptians into confusion and caused the wheels of the chariots to fall off.

With the Israelites safely settled on the other side of the Red Sea, God gave Moses some further instructions...

STRETCH OUT YOUR HAND OVER THE SEA SO THAT THE WATERS MAY FLOW BACK OVER THE EGYPTIANS AND THEIR CHARIOTS AND THEIR MEN.

The Bible tells us that at daybreak, Moses did as God commanded and Pharaoh's entire army was drowned.

Boring Bible Fact: In the Hebrew language the Red Sea is actually called the REED Sea!

Moses The Singer

Moses and the Israelites couldn't believe their eyes.
At last they were free from hundreds of years of slavery.
Moses just couldn't contain his excitement any longer.
Moses did what countless other people have done through the years when they've wanted a satisfactory way of expressing their feelings.
He sang a song.

There's loads more verses to this song but don't worry, we're not going to listen to Moses sing all of it but you could always check it out in Exodus chapter 15.

If you're musical yourself, why not have a go at composing a tune for it?

All the Israelites joined in Moses' song of praise to the God who had saved them and I reckon *we* would as well if *we'd* just been rescued in such a dramatic and spectacular way.

Boring Bible Joke:
Why did Moses always carry a comb with him?
For the PARTING of the Red Sea!

The Israelites' joy soon turned to anger when, after walking for three days into the desert, they started to run out of water.
They stopped at a place called Marah but they couldn't drink the water because it tasted bitter.

It didn't take long for Moses to turn from being their hero to the villain of the peace.

Moses cried out to God for a solution and God told him to throw a piece of wood into the bitter water and miraculously it became sweet.
God also made a bargain with the Israelites at Marah.

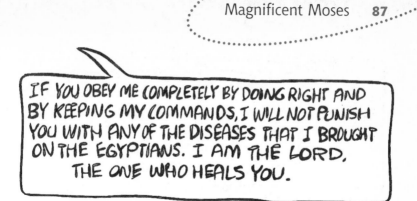

IF YOU OBEY ME COMPLETELY BY DOING RIGHT AND BY KEEPING MY COMMANDS, I WILL NOT PUNISH YOU WITH ANY OF THE DISEASES THAT I BROUGHT ON THE EGYPTIANS. I AM THE LORD, THE ONE WHO HEALS YOU.

Seems fair enough to me, but you're going to have to keep an eye on the Israelites and check out whether they keep *their* side of the bargain.

Keep reading and you'll soon find out!

Grumble, Grumble, Grumble!

One month into their freedom the Israelites were beginning to wish they'd never left Egypt.

Even with their livestock, there wasn't enough food to go round.

BACK IN EGYPT WE HAD ALL THE FOOD WE COULD EVER WISH FOR!

What a load of moaning minnies the Israelites were.

If they kept walking at the same rate they'd be arriving at the wonderful new land that God had promised them in maybe just a few months.

God had promised that the land they were going to would be overflowing with good things *and* they'd be free from slavery. What more could they ask for?

But God was patient with the Israelites and told Moses that he would supply all the food the two million Israelites needed until they reached the Promised Land. Seems a bit of a tall order to me.

I wonder how God was going to do it...?

Well, not like *that*, that's for sure!

Mind Your Mannas!

Here's what God did.
God told Moses...

> I AM GOING TO MAKE FOOD RAIN DOWN FROM THE SKY FOR ALL OF YOU. THE PEOPLE MUST GO OUT EVERY DAY AND GATHER ENOUGH FOR THAT DAY. IN THIS WAY I CAN TEST THEM TO FIND OUT IF THEY WILL FOLLOW MY INSTRUCTIONS. ON THE SIXTH DAY THEY ARE TO BRING IN TWICE AS MUCH AS USUAL.

What do *you* reckon?
Will the grumbling Israelites pass God's test and do exactly what he says or will they disobey him?

☐ YES   ☐ NO

Moses told Aaron to tell the Israelites that God would give them bread in the morning and meat in the evening.
That Moses! He *still* doesn't like public speaking, does he?
As the entire Israelite population waited in the desert, a dazzling light appeared before them. It was God himself. Awesome!
God wanted them to know that their grumbling had reached his ears and now he was going to prove to them that he was indeed their God.

I wonder what was going through their minds as they waited to see the miracle that God was going to perform?
As evening approached, they were about to find out.

Did you guess that the Israelites would disobey God sooner or later?

If you did then you'd be right.

Some of them chose to completely ignore what Moses had said and kept back some of their manna for the next morning.

All week long the Israelites enjoyed their tasty new food and everyone had enough to eat. As the sun grew hot each day, the manna that was left over melted. On the sixth day of the week Moses gave them some more instructions...

Do You Remember?... If you've read the Boring Bible book,
***Ballistic Beginnings* then you'll probably remember how**
God created the world in six days and then rested on the
seventh day.
God commanded Abraham and all his descendants to do
the same so they could take time out to worship him as
well as rest from their work.

Amazingly, this time, the manna did not go rotten the next day.
God had preserved it.
But still some of the Israelites chose to disobey God's
instructions.
God had told them not to leave their homes but...
God's patience was certainly being sorely tried.

Boring Bible Fact: God commanded Moses to put a jar-full
of manna into a special wooden chest that would be kept
so that future generations would be able to see the
miracles God had performed.

Manna would be what the Israelites ate for the next 40 years as they wandered in the desert.

But hang on a minute. I thought you said they be in the land got had promised them in a matter of *months*?

Stick with me and all will be revealed.

Time To Go!

At God's command the Israelites moved from place to place. Even as they left the Desert of Sin and arrived at Rephidim they were back to their grumbling old ways.

Once again, God patiently gave them what they wanted.

Water, On The Rocks, Please!

God told Moses that he would produce water from a rock at Mount Sinai.

Miraculously, the Israelites had their thirst quenched.

Did you know...the Bible calls the Israelites a 'stiff-necked people' which meant that they didn't take too kindly to being told what to do by God?

They were forever finding *something* to grumble about.

**Because of their rebellious attitude towards God's
goodness only two of them ever made it into the land that
God had promised.**

**Except for Joshua and Caleb, everyone over the age of
twenty was now condemned to wander around in the
desert for 40 years until they'd died and a new generation
of Israelites had grown up.**

Now, we've got a bit of a choice here.

We can either follow the Israelites through their *entire* 40 years
of wanderings, which is going to be a bit boring, and will
probably make this book about ten times as big as it is at the
moment, or we can just have a look at the edited highlights.

Okay, let's take a vote.

Right, that's agreed then.

THE BORING BIBLE
PROUDLY PRESENTS
THE EDITED HIGHLIGHTS
OF THE ISRAELITES'
40 YEARS OF WANDERING
IN THE DESERT

EDITED HIGHLIGHTS NO.1
THE ADVENTURES OF MOUNT SINAI

Exactly three months to the day since they'd left Egypt, the Israelites came to Mount Sinai, othewise known as the holy mountain of God.

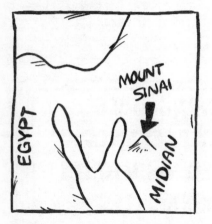

Can you remember back to the early part of this book when God promised Moses that one of the signs he would give him that the Israelites would be freed from slavery in Egypt was that they would one day come to Mount Sinai to worship him? Well, that day had finally arrived.

While the Israelites camped at the foot of the mountain, Moses went up it to meet with God.

The Bible tells us what God said...

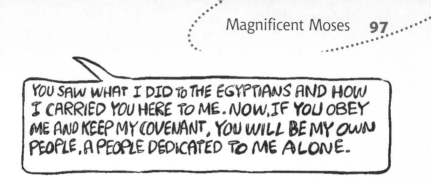

YOU SAW WHAT I DID TO THE EGYPTIANS AND HOW I CARRIED YOU HERE TO ME. NOW, IF YOU OBEY ME AND KEEP MY COVENANT, YOU WILL BE MY OWN PEOPLE, A PEOPLE DEDICATED TO ME ALONE.

Boring Bible Fact: A covenant is another name for a promise or an agreement.

Moses went back to the Israelites and told them what God had said.

WE **WILL** DO EVERYTHING THE LORD HAS SAID.

Moses went back up the mountain to give their reply to God.

I AM GOING TO COME TO YOU IN A THICK CLOUD SO THAT THE PEOPLE WILL HEAR ME SPEAKING WITH YOU AND WILL PUT THEIR TRUST IN YOU FROM NOW ON.

God instructed the Israelites to get themselves ready for meeting him by purifying themselves. That means getting themselves cleaned up.

Moses was also told to mark out a boundary line round the foot of the mountain. If anybody crossed over it they must be put to death immediately. God was making sure that they took meeting him seriously.

ARE YOU GOING TO BE IN THERE ALL DAY? YOU'RE NOT THE ONLY ONE WHO NEEDS PURIFYING!

BATHROOM.

The Israelites had seen God's power with the plagues in Egypt and also the miraculous crossing of the Red Sea. The thought of now *meeting* this awesome God scared them witless. They were petrified. As the time ticked by the atmosphere was getting increasingly tense.

Three days had passed, and just when they were getting to the point where they couldn't stand the waiting any longer, a trumpet blast sounded throughout the camp.

This was the signal they had been waiting for. The time had arrived to meet God.

The Bible says that the people trembled with fear.

Before their very eyes smoke covered Mount Sinai.

The Israelites legs' were turning to jelly.

The trumpet sound was getting louder.

As Moses went up the mountain, God spoke to him with a voice that sounded like thunder...

I AM THE LORD YOUR GOD WHO BROUGHT YOU OUT OF EGYPT WHERE YOU WERE SLAVES.

Then God instructed Moses to tell the Israelites ten things that they either must or mustn't do.

These have come to be known as the Ten Commandments and they were God's way of making certain that the Israelites kept themselves from going the same way as all the other nations who were evil and wicked and did just what they pleased. Here's what God commanded them...

1 Don't worship any other gods except me.
2 Don't make idols and give them your worship instead of me. I don't tolerate rivals. Put me first.
3 Do not misuse my name or use it as a swear word.
4 Work six days and then set aside the seventh day of the week to worship me.
5 Respect your parents and then I will give you a long life.
6 Do not murder anyone.
7 Do not have sex with someone who isn't your husband or wife.
8 Do not steal.
9 Do not lie against somebody else.
10 Do not be envious of what other people have got and then set your heart on getting it.

God also gave the Israelites lots of other laws and instructions to make sure they enjoyed a good life.

Moses wasn't the only one to see God face to face.

Aaron and the other leaders of the Israelites were also permitted by God to enter the cloud where he was.

The Bible describes what they saw...

'Beneath God's feet was what looked like a pavement of sapphire as blue as the sky.'

Moses once more ascended the mountain and went into the very presence of God himself.

God handed Moses two stone tablets (that's 'flat stones' to you and me), on which he had personally written all the laws and commands he'd given to the Israelites.

Boring Bible Fact: People often think that the two stone tablets just had the Ten Commandments on them and nothing else but the Bible actually says that it had on it all the laws and instructions that he'd given the Israelites.

Moses was up the mountain with God for 40, that's nearly six weeks, and the Israelites were beginning to wonder whether they'd ever see him again.
At last, they decided that they were fed up waiting and got together with Aaron to make a gold bull-calf idol to worship out of all their gold jewellery.

Hang on a minute!
Wasn't one of the Ten Commandments something about *not* making idols?

When Moses eventually returned he was furious.
He was so angry that he smashed the two stone tablets that God had given him.
Moses melted down the gold calf, then ground it down to a fine powder, mixed it with water and made the rebellious Israelites drink it.

Did you know... God gave Moses another pair of stone tablets with his laws and instructions to replace the one Moses had broken?

God planned to stay with the Israelites wherever they went so he instructed Moses to built a portable building, like a tent, that would be used as a special place to worship him.

One day, when the Israelites finally settled in the Promised Land, they would be able to build a permanent temple out of stone but until that day, the tabernacle, as it was called, would be where God was worshipped.

God gave Moses instructions of exactly how he wanted the tabernacle to be built, down to the very last gold hook and tent pole.

It looked something like this...

Turn over to page 104 for a diagram of the tabernacle.

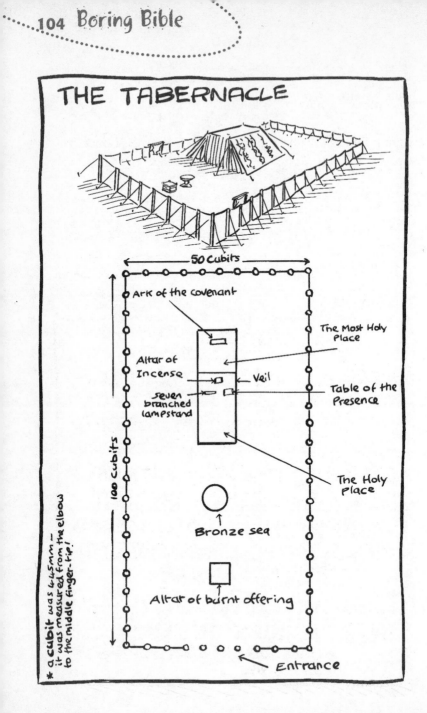

THE TABERNACLE

50 Cubits

100 Cubits

Ark of the covenant

The Most Holy Place

Altar of Incense

Veil

Table of the Presence

seven branched lampstand

The Holy Place

Bronze sea

Altar of burnt offering

Entrance

* a cubit was 445mm – it was measured from the elbow to the middle finger-tip!

When the tabernacle was complete, the cloud of God's presence came down and filled it. So powerful was God's presence that even Moses couldn't enter the tent.

Boring Bible Fact: Up until now the Israelites had been carrying around Moses' miraculous staff and a jar of manna in a not-too-fancy box.
There were now also the two stone tablets to be carried around so God told Moses to build a very special box or ark, to keep them in. It's sometimes called the Covenant Box or the Ark of the Covenant. If you've seen the film *Indiana Jones and the Temple of Doom* **you will have seen a fictional story about a race to discover its whereabouts.**

JOB VACANCY

WE'RE LOOKING FOR PEOPLE TO CARRY THE TABERNACLE OF GOD, ALONG WITH ITS FURNITURE, CURTAINS AND COVERINGS. YOU'LL ALSO HAVE TO DO ALL THE DAY-TO-DAY MENIAL JOBS AROUND THE TABERNACLE SO YOU'LL HAVE TO ENJOY BEING A BACKROOM BOY.

A GOOD SINGING VOICE WOULDN'T GO AMISS BECAUSE YOU'LL SOMETIMES BE EXPECTED TO LEAD WORSHIP.

NO PREVIOUS EXPERIENCE NECESSARY.
SALARY:- THE REST OF THE ISRAELITES WILL GIVE YOU ONE TENTH OF THEIR INCOME.

The tribe that God gave this job to were the Levites.
Originally, there were twelve tribes of Israel who were all
descendants of the sons of Jacob.
(Remember Jacob from Boring Bible book *Hotchpotch Hebrews*?)
Because God had set aside the Levites to serve him in the
tabernacle that meant they couldn't fight for Israel or own land
when they arrived in Canaan, God's promised land, which is
what the twelve tribes were expected to do.
So the Levites were dropped from being one of Israel's twelve
tribes.

For that matter, so was
Joseph, who also featured in
Hotchpotch Hebrews.

Joseph's sons, Ephraim and Manasseh made up the numbers instead.
Just in case your were wondering who the other ten tribes were, here's the full list: Reuben, Simeon, Judah, Issachar, Zebulun, Benjamin, Dan, Asher, Gad, Naphtali, Ephraim and Manasseh.

JOB VACANCY

WE'RE LOOKING FOR PEOPLE WHO DON'T MIND THE SIGHT OF BLOOD AND WHO ALSO DON'T MIND WEARING EXTRAVAGANT CLOTHING. YOU'RE GOING TO BE THE GO-BETWEENS FOR THE ISRAELITES AND GOD. ONCE A YEAR YOU MIGHT EVEN BE CHOSEN TO MEET GOD HIMSELF!

WOULD SUIT PEOPLE WHO AREN'T SQUEAMISH OR FAINT-HEARTED.

PERKS INCLUDE A SHARE OF THE SACRIFICES.

UNIFORM SUPPLIED.

APPLY **NOW**!

Priests were chosen to work inside the tabernacle making sacrifices to God. Aaron's family got the job and a smelly, dirty job it was too.

You're most probably wondering why on earth animals had to be killed and sacrificed to God, so let me tell you.

Sacrifices are all about giving to God something that we own. Making a sacrifice wasn't a way of getting into God's good books.

The Israelites were required to do it simply to make peace with God.

It was what God told them to do.

In Boring Bible book *Ballistic Beginnings* we saw how Adam and Eve, God's first two people, sinned against God by disobeying him and doing as they pleased. Since then the Bible says that all people have been affected by sin and although the Israelites' sacrifices could get them pardoned for doing certain things wrong no amount of sacrificed animals could wipe away sin itself which caused them to do wrong.

**Boring Bible Book Advance Warning!...Get a copy of
Boring Bible book *Super Son* and find out whose sacrifice
really *can* get rid of sin for good!**

Here are some of the different sorts of sacrifices the priests had
to make...

Burnt-offering

Get one whole animal (skinned) and place your hands on it to
show that it was a sacrifice for your failings. Be sure that the
animal is perfect. (Only the best is good enough for God!)
Sprinkle the blood of the animal on the altar as a sign that the
life of the animal has been given to God.

Grain-offering

This sacrifice was intended to make sure that God didn't forget
you.
Flour, grain and baked cakes or raw grain, oil and frankincense
was your way of making a goodwill offering to God.

Sin-offering

If you have sinned against God or another person then this
one's for you. Because your sin has contaminated the holy
tabernacle it needs to be cleansed. Sprinkle the blood of an
animal to do the job. Some of the animal's meat was given to
the priest to eat. If it didn't do him any harm it meant that God
had accepted your sacrifice and that you were now off the hook.

At long last, the land of Canaan, which God had promised them to live in, was within sight. Moses was ready to march on in and conquer it for God but suddenly fear crept through the Israelite camp.

Moses agreed to their request and chose one man from each tribe and sent them off into the new land as spies.
40 days later they returned but it wasn't good news...

Caleb, one of the twelve, couldn't believe what scaredy-cats they were!

Nobody but Moses and Aaron would listen to him.
They were back to their old moaning, grumbling ways.
Can you believe it, after all they'd seen God do for them?

The Bible says that they even wanted to choose a new leader for themselves and head back to Egypt!

The Israelites did, in fact, realise that they'd made a big mistake, but it was too late for God to change his mind.
Against Moses' advice they decided that on second thoughts they would invade the land of Canaan after all but because neither Moses or God was with them they were defeated big time.

So that was that.
For the next 38 years, the Israelites wandered around the desert, occasionally bumping into some of the nations that they would one day conquer, which I suppose was good training for the Israelite army.

As we've already mentioned, the whole story of Moses and the Israelites' wanderings in the desert comes from four books in the Bible: Exodus, Leviticus, Numbers and Deuteronomy.

Most of it was taken out of **Exodus**, but in case you're wondering what stuff was in the other three, **Leviticus** tells us everything we'll ever need to know about the Levites and the sacrifices that the Israelites had to make.

Numbers is a bit like a census where every single person in a country is counted. Moses had the Israelites counted so he knew what size army he'd have to fight the people of Canaan.

Deuteronomy is Moses' farewell speech to the Israelites before he died.

Moses reminds them all about God's promises and God's instructions.

Why didn't *Moses* make it into the land of Canaan?

After all that Moses had done for God you'd have thought he'd at least be allowed to enter Canaan, but no. Way back at Meribah, when God had given the Israelites water from the rock, Moses lost his temper with his grumbling people and didn't do exactly what God had told him to do. This is what God said...

BECAUSE YOU DID NOT HAVE ENOUGH FAITH TO ACKNOWLEDGE MY HOLY POWER BEFORE THE PEOPLE OF ISRAEL, YOU WILL NOT LEAD THEM INTO THE LAND I PROMISED TO GIVE THEM.

The Bible says that before Moses died at the ripe old age of 120, he went to Mount Nebo and God showed him the land that would one day be home to the Israelites.

And so, Moses died.

You'll have to read Boring Bible book, *Catastrophic Kings* to find out what happened when the Israelites finally entered Canaan and the many adventures that they had there.

One thing I *can* tell you and that is that good old Joshua, Moses right-hand man, took over being leader of the Israelites and what a fine leader he turned out to be.

The Bit at the End

Here are some reminders of some of the stuff we've had a look at in Magnificent Moses.

What's Been Happening?

Moses is born. (His family are Israelite slaves.)

Moses sails up Nile, single-handed, in a reed basket.

Moses rescued by Pharaoh's daughter and brought up as an Egyptian prince.

Moses kills an Egyptian and does a runner to Midian.

Moses becomes a shepherd and marries Zipporah.

God appears to Moses in a burning bush and tells him to go back to Egypt to free the Israelites.

Moses goes back to Egypt with his brother Aaron.

Moses tries to persuade Pharaoh to let the Israelites go (with a little help from a bunch of rather nasty plagues).

Pharaoh eventually gives in.

The Israelites flee.

Pharaoh changes his mind and goes after them.

God parts the Red Sea so the Israelites can cross but the Egyptians get drowned.

God provides manna and quail and water for the Israelites.

Moses meets God at Mount Sinai and gets given the Ten Commandments.

Tabernacle built for God.

Israelites moan and grumble.

40 years of wandering in desert (with a lot more moaning and grumbling).

Moses dies and Joshua takes over.

A Quick Run-Down Of The Main Characters

Moses (Hebrew name Manasseh).
Moses' mum.
Miriam (Moses' sister).
Pharaoh's daughter.
Pharaoh (a few of them actually).
Lots of Israelite slaves.
Lots of Egyptian slave-drivers.
Jethro.
Zipporah (Mrs Moses).
Aaron (Moses' brother).
Joshua and Caleb.
And as always...God!

Your Turn

Write down any bits of the Bible that you don't think are quite so boring any more...

Don't forget, you can read all of these stories and loads of other amazing ones in a proper Bible. *That* way you'll find out what bits we didn't have space for in this book. There's some great Bibles around just for kids, so why not try and get your hands on one?
Have fun!

HERE ARE **SOME** BITESIZE -BITS- OF THE BIBLE

(JUST TO GIVE YOU A TASTE OF A **REAL** BIBLE!)

GO ON— HAVE A NIBBLE!

One day while Moses was taking care of the sheep and goats of his father-in-law Jethro, the priest of Midian, he led the flock across the desert and came to Sinai, the holy mountain. There the angel of the Lord appeared to him as a flame coming from the middle of a bush.

Exodus 3: 1 - 2

'CHEW!

'SLURP!

Then Moses and Aaron went to the king of Egypt and said, "The Lord, the God of Israel, says, 'Let my people go, so that they can hold a festival in the desert to honour me.'"

Exodus 5: 1

MUNCH!

CHOMP!

At midnight the Lord killed all the first-born sons in Egypt, from the king's son, who was heir to the throne, to the son of the prisoner in the dungeon; all the first-born animals were also killed.

Exodus 12: 29

CHEW!

MUNCH!

CHOMP!

Moses held out his hand over the sea, and the Lord drove the sea back with a strong east wind. It blew all night and turned the sea into dry land. The water was divided, and the Israelites went through the sea on dry ground, with walls of water on both sides.

Exodus 14: 21 - 22

NIBBLE!

SLURP!

God spoke, and these were his words:
"I am the Lord your God who brought you out of Egypt, where you were slaves. Worship no god but me."

Exodus 20: 1 - 2

CHEW!

MUNCH!

CHOMP!

The Lord said to Moses, "I now make a covenant with the people of Israel. In their presence I will do great things such as have never been done anywhere on earth among any of the nations."

Exodus 34: 10

NIBBLE!

CHEW!

SLURP!

"If you live according to my laws and obey my commands, I will send you rain at the right time, so that the land will produce crops and the trees bear fruit. Your crops will be so plentiful that you will be harvesting corn when it is time to pick grapes, and you will still be picking grapes when it is time to sow corn. You will have what you want to eat, and you will live in safety in your land."

Leviticus 26: 3 - 5

CHOMP!

MUNCH!

CHEW!

"The Lord your God will lead you, and he will fight for you, just as you saw him do in Egypt and in the desert. You saw how he brought you safely all the way to this place, just as a father would carry his son."

Deuteronomy 1: 30 - 31

MUNCH!

NIBBLE!

SLURP!

"Today I am giving you a choice between good and evil, between life and death. If you obey the commands of the Lord your God, which I give you today, if you love him, obey him, and keep all his laws, then you will prosper and become a nation of many people."

Deuteronomy 30: 15 - 16

CHEW!

MUNCH!

CHOMP!

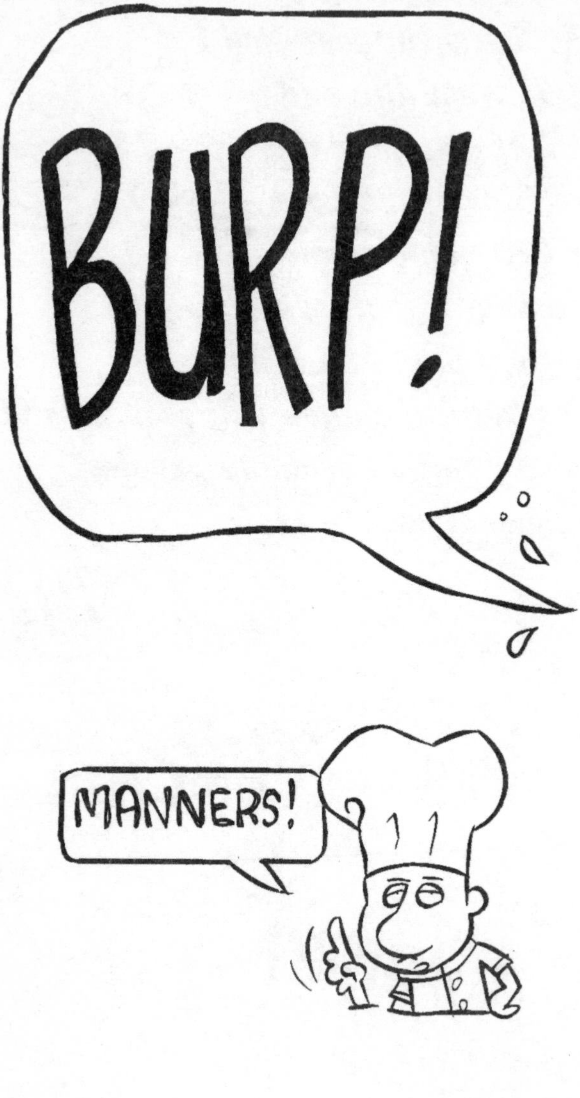
BURP!
MANNERS!